NEW MEXICO STATE UNIVERSITY
&
DONA ANA COMMUNITY COLLEGE

STUDENT
RESOURCE BOOK

A QUICK & USEFUL GUIDE TO NMSU AND DACC CAMPUS RESOURCES

PHILIP HERNANDEZ

TABLE OF CONTENTS

NEW MEXICO STATE UNIVERSITY

RESOURCES

NEW MEXICO STATE UNIVERSITY
WRITING CENTER

LOCATION

Main Campus
Clara Belle Williams Hall Room 102

HOURS

Hours vary. Check website for hours.

COST | ELIGIBILITY

Undergraduate and graduate students of any discipline.

SERVICES PROVIDED Provides one-on-one writing consultation, feedback and brainstorming assistance on any writing assignment for all undergraduate and graduate students.

Help students become more knowledgeable, practiced, and confident writers through collaborative, dialogue-centered consultations.

NEW MEXICO STATE UNIVERSITY
MATH SUCCESS CENTER

LOCATION

Main Campus
Walden Hall Room 101

HOURS

Monday-Thursday: 9am-2pm
Friday: 9am-12pm

COST | ELIGIBILITY

Free to any NMSU Student who has taken a Math course

SERVICES PROVIDED Provides tutoring for all math undergraduate courses, with special focus on services for students enrolled in Math 111, 120, 121 or 190.

NEW MEXICO STATE UNIVERSITY

ZUHL LIBRARY COPY CENTER

LOCATION

Zuhl Library 1st Floor

COST | ELIGIBILITY

Microfilm/fiche printing/scanning: $0.10/page with library copy card or cash.

Free of charge if saved to your USB drive or emailed.

SERVICES PROVIDED

•Fast, cost-effective and high quality document duplication and finishing service.
•Faxing (send or receive)
•Copying with collated and staple options
•Image reduction and enlargement
•Lamination
•Photocopying of personal and library materials
•Transparencies
black and white or color

HOURS

Fall and Spring

Sun: 10 am - 12 am
Mon-Thurs: 7:30am - 12 am
Fri: 7:30am - 8pm
Sat: 9am - 6pm

Summer

Sun: Closed
Mon-Thurs: 7:30am - 9pm
Fri: 7:30am - 6pm
Sat: 10am - 6pm

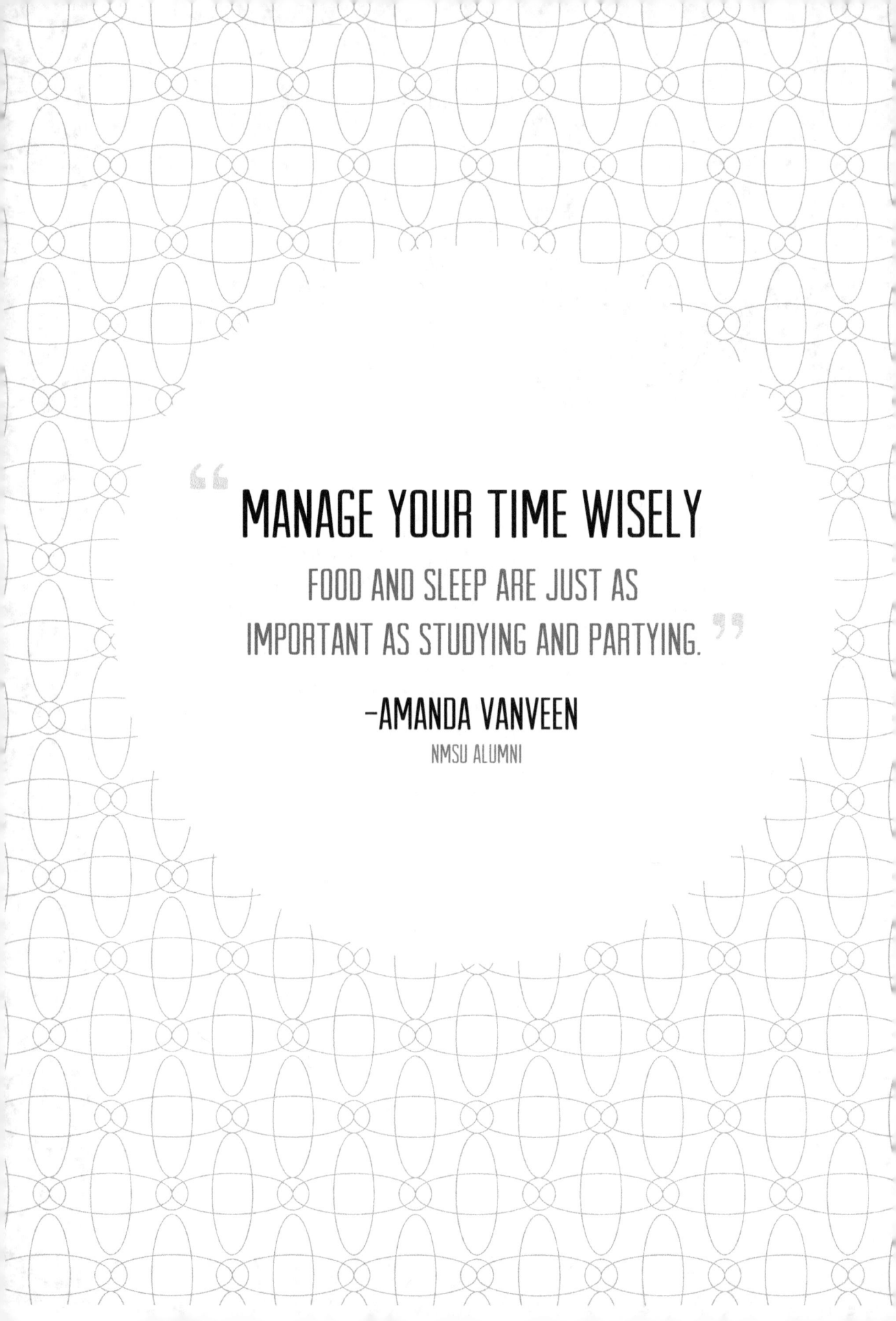

" "

MANAGE YOUR TIME WISELY

FOOD AND SLEEP ARE JUST AS
IMPORTANT AS STUDYING AND PARTYING. " "

–AMANDA VANVEEN

NMSU ALUMNI

NEW MEXICO STATE UNIVERSITY
STUDENT HEALTH CENTER

LOCATION

Main Campus
Corner of McFie and Breland, across the
street from Zuhl Library

HOURS

Monday - Friday
7:30am - 11:30am
1pm - 4pm
Year Round

SERVICES PROVIDED
Offers out-patient primary health care with a staff of physicians, nurse
practitioners, and other health care professionals. Medical specialty services
include nutrition and mental health services.

NEW MEXICO STATE UNIVERSITY
BLACK PROGRAMS

LOCATION

Main Campus
Garcia Annex Room 135

HOURS

Each program has different hours

COST | ELIGIBILITY

All students are eligible to use services

SERVICES PROVIDED
Counseling and academic assistance; maintains a library of Black Studies
materials; sponsors cultural and social events for students; and assists with
job placement and job referrals.

NEW MEXICO STATE UNIVERSITY

STUDENT JUDICIAL AFFAIRS

LOCATION

Main Campus
Corbett Center Suite 230

HOURS

Monday - Friday: 8am - 5pm

COST | ELIGIBILITY

Any student who is the student of NMSU is eligible.

If any student is having problem with other student or he/she is in trouble can use the service.

SERVICES PROVIDED Office maintains all student records relating to both academic and non-academic student misconduct as well as databases of publications relating to student conduct issues.

NEW MEXICO STATE UNIVERSITY

INDIAN RESOURCE
DEVELOPMENT PROGRAM

LOCATION

Main Campus
Gerald Thomas Hall Room 263

SERVICES PROVIDED Helps tribal students through a variety of professional development activities.

NEW MEXICO STATE UNIVERSITY

STUDENT SUPPORT SERVICES
TRIO PROGRAM (SSS)

LOCATION
Main Campus
Hardman Hall Room 210

HOURS
Monday - Friday: 8am - 5pm

COST | ELIGIBILITY

•A U.S. Citizen or permanent resident.
•Enrolled full-time and are degree seeking on the NMSU - Main Campus.
•Freshman, Sophomore, or Transfer student.
•Demonstrate Academic Need.
•First generation college student (Neither parent graduated from college or university with a Bachelor's Degree).
•Meet specific U.S. Department of Education income guidelines.
•A documented learning disability or physical disability and are registered with Services for Students with Disabilities Office.

SERVICES PROVIDED Provides academic assistance to participants. Assistance includes mentoring, tutoring, academic and financial aid advising. To be eligible, students must meet first generation and federal income guidelines or be a student with a disability and be registered with the SSD office at NMSU.

NEW MEXICO STATE UNIVERSITY

CRIMSON SCHOLARS

LOCATION

Main Campus
Conroy Honors Building Room 104

HOURS

Monday - Friday: 8am - 4pm

COST | ELIGIBILITY

Students who have a cumulative 3.5 GPA and are taking three or more credits per semester.

SERVICES PROVIDED Students who qualify are eligible for: Honors classes, early registration, Crimson Scholars advising and extended library check out periods.

NEW MEXICO STATE UNIVERSITY

STUDY ABROAD OFFICE

LOCATION

Main Campus
Garcia Annex Room 238

HOURS

8am - 4pm
Schedule appointment only

COST | ELIGIBILITY

All enrolled students who receive Financial Aid are eligible.

SERVICES PROVIDED To help students who are interested in other cultures, other countries, languages, or even just want to be successful on a global scale.

COOPERATIVE EDUCATION

LOCATION

Main Campus
Garcia Annex 2nd Floor Room 224

HOURS

8am - 4pm

SERVICES PROVIDED Plans include alternating (full-time, often multiple experiences) or parallel (part-time experience concurrent with full-time school).

"

THERE ARE SO MANY PEOPLE ON THIS CAMPUS WHO WANT YOU TO SUCCEED...

SEEK THEM OUT!

TALK TO THEM IF YOU ARE HAVING PROBLEMS OR CONCERNS. AND
NEXT YEAR, BE ONE OF THOSE PEOPLE FOR THE NEW FRESHMEN!

"

-SHARON M. NELSON-HAMMERSMITH

NMSU ALUMNI

NEW MEXICO STATE UNIVERSITY

AQUATIC CENTER

LOCATION

Stewart Street between Locust and Williams Avenue

HOURS

Monday - Friday: 6am - 9pm
Saturday: 7am - 7pm
Sunday: 12pm - 5pm

Check website for pool schedules

SERVICES PROVIDED

The NMSU Aquatic Center contains a 25-yard indoor pool and an Olympic-size outdoor pool. Both pools are heated and are open all year round. Come swim laps or go off the 1 meter or 3 meter diving boards during our recreation time.

WONDERS OF

NMSU

NEW MEXICO STATE UNIVERSITY
FAMILY RESOURCE CENTER

LOCATION

4145 Sam Steel Way
Las Cruces, NM
88003
C-100 Cervantes
Village (Near
Children's Village)

HOURS

Mon: 9am - 5pm
Tues: 9am -12:30pm
      2:30pm - 5pm
Wed: 9am -5pm
Thurs: 11am - 2pm
Fri-Sun: Closed

COST | ELIGIBILITY

NMSU or DACC
Students

SERVICES PROVIDED

- Toddler Time
- Preschool Play
- After School

Program
- Fun Family
Activities

- Marriage and
Family Therapy
- Nutritional Services

- Family Referral
Services
- Back Packs for Kids

NEW MEXICO STATE UNIVERSITY
UNIVERSITY MUSEUM

LOCATION

Kent Hall, MSC
3564, Las Cruces,
NM 88003-88001

HOURS

Tuesday - Saturday:
12pm - 4pm

COST | ELIGIBILITY

Open to the public

SERVICES PROVIDED

- Offer facility to
graduates for their
research

- Exhibits
- Family workshop

NEW MEXICO STATE UNIVERSITY
CENTER FOR THE ARTS

LOCATION

Main Campus
Corner of University
and Espina

HOURS

Monday - Saturday:
8am - 8pm

COST | ELIGIBILITY

Visit the website
for complete ticket
information.

SERVICES PROVIDED

Providing opportunity for arts and performing arts to centrally
locate their talent, including but not limited to Theatre, Dance,
Orchestra, Artist, and other Performing Arts

NEW MEXICO STATE UNIVERSITY
CREATIVE MEDIA INSTITUTE

LOCATION

Main Campus
2915 McFie Circle
Milton Hall
Room 172B
Las Cruces, NM
88003

HOURS

Monday - Friday:
8am - 12pm
1pm - 5pm

SERVICES PROVIDED

Curriculum focuses on the art, craft, and business of storytelling,
Digital Arts, Digital Filmmaking, Animation & Visual Effects.

BARNES & NOBLE CAFE

LOCATION

1400 E. University
Las Cruces, NM
88003

HOURS

Monday - Friday:
7:30am - 8pm
Saturday:
10am - 6pm
Sunday:
11am - 5pm

SERVICES PROVIDED

- Course Bookstore
- Apparel Store
- Accessories

- Starbucks
- Convenient Store located inside

- Comfortable and quiet Café

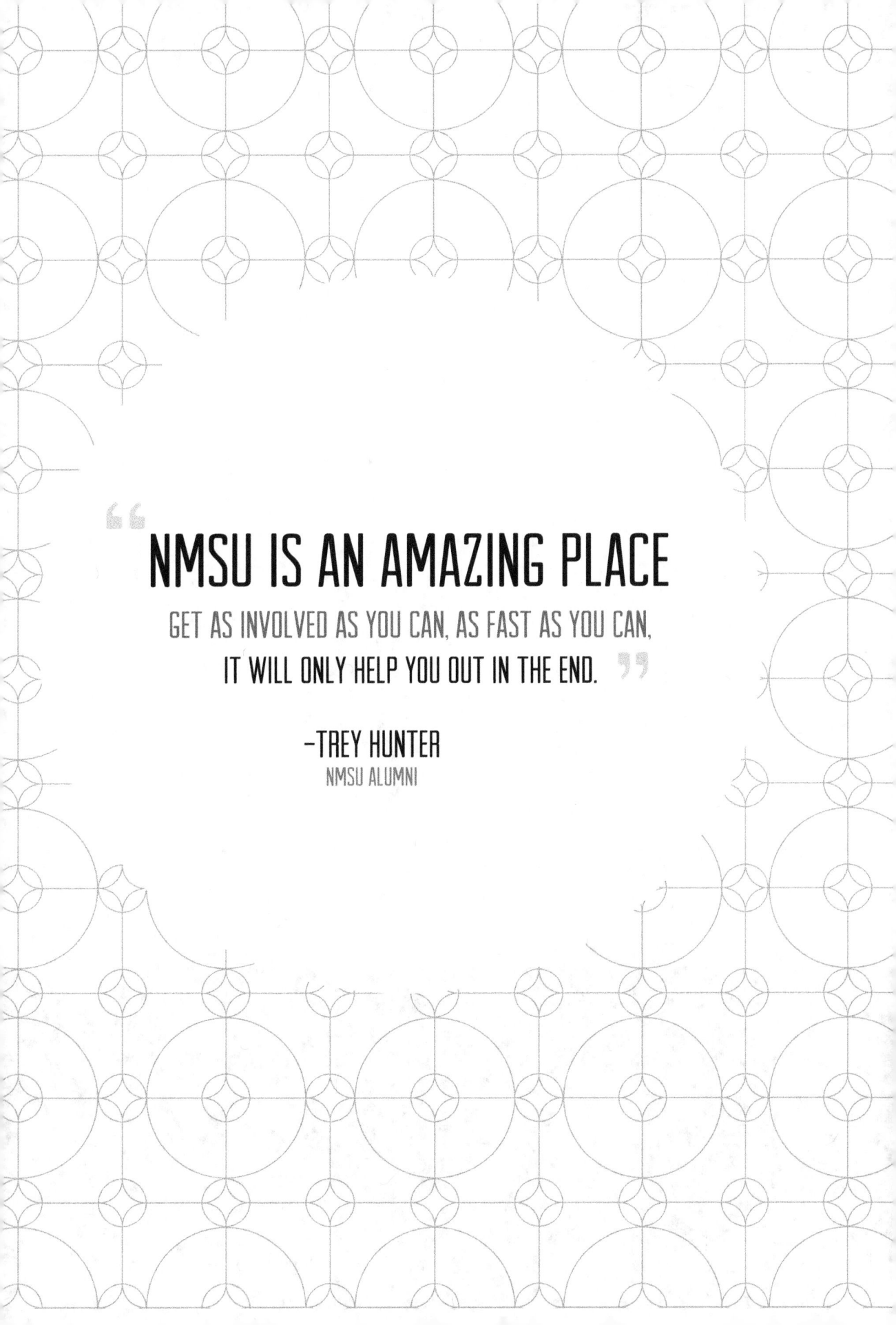

"

NMSU IS AN AMAZING PLACE

GET AS INVOLVED AS YOU CAN, AS FAST AS YOU CAN,
IT WILL ONLY HELP YOU OUT IN THE END. "

-TREY HUNTER
NMSU ALUMNI

DONA ANA COMMUNITY COLLEGE

RESOURCES

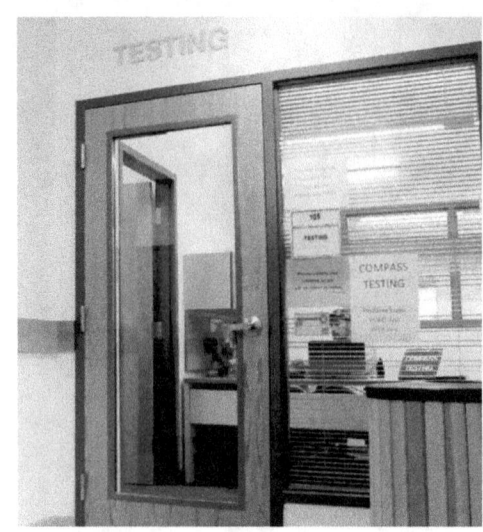

DONA ANA COMMUNITY COLLEGE

STUDENT RESOURCE TESTING CENTER

LOCATION

East Mesa Campus
DASR Room 105

HOURS

Monday - Friday:
8am - 12pm
1pm - 5pm

COST | ELIGIBILITY

$10.00 per test ($50.00 for the battery).

SERVICES PROVIDED
Offers information and administers a variety of State and National exams and a test environment free of distractions and intimidation.

- GED
- ACT/ACT Residual
- CHES Exam
- CLEP Exam

- COMPASS Assessment
- GMAT
- GRE
- HOBET

- LSAT
- Math Placement
- MCAT
- Miller Analogies
- NMTA

- Pearson VUE
- PRAXIS
- Proctored Exams
- TOEFL ITP

DONA ANA COMMUNITY COLLEGE
DUAL CREDIT OFFICE

LOCATION

East Mesa Campus
DASR Room 101 B

HOURS

Monday-Friday: 8am - 5pm

COST | ELIGIBILITY

•Be a high school junior or senior
•Be enrolled at least half-time in a school district that has a Dual Credit agreement with DACC
•Maintain a minimum high school grade point average of 2.0
•Pass two of three areas of the COMPASS test OR have an ACT composite of 15
•Maintain a minimum grade point average of 2.0 in your dual credit courses to continue in the program.

SERVICES PROVIDED
High school students may gain college credit while in high school.

DONA ANA COMMUNITY COLLEGE
LIBRARY & MEDIA CENTER

LOCATION

Central Campus: Room 260 (2nd Floor of the Learning Resources Bldg.)

HOURS

Monday-Friday: 8am - 5pm

COST | ELIGIBILITY

All students currently enrolled in DACC

SERVICES PROVIDED
Offers research assistance for faculty staff and students, information on literacy program for students, computer for students to complete assignments and tutoring services.

> "**TAKE IT**
> IF YOU ARE SCARED TO DO
> **DO IT**
> ENJOY THE 4 YEARS YOU ARE

ALL IN.

SOMETHING, OR JOIN A GROUP,

ANYWAY.

HERE BEFORE THEY ARE GONE. "

-STEPHANIE
NMSU ALUMNI

DONA ANA COMMUNITY COLLEGE
COUNSELING & WELLNESS CENTER

LOCATION
DACC Main building Room 117

HOURS
Monday-Thursday: 8am - 5pm
Appointments for regular sessions are made between 9 am and 3 pm.

COST | ELIGIBILITY
Students must currently be enrolled at DACC

SERVICES PROVIDED Counseling can lead to improved academic performance, better interpersonal relationships, reduction of stress and strategies and tools for the solution and management of specific problems and solutions. Offers individual, couples, and group brief integrative counseling. Allows individuals to discuss personal issues that can produce uncomfortable feelings.

DONA ANA COMMUNITY COLLEGE
FINANCIAL AID & SCHOLARSHIPS

LOCATION
Gerald Thomas Hall Room 308

HOURS
Monday-Friday: 8am - 5pm

COST | ELIGIBILITY
Cost of Attendance is the estimate of expenses you meet in order to attend.

SERVICES PROVIDED Provides financial advice and resources to help students with: grants, loans, work-study and scholarships.

DONA ANA COMMUNITY COLLEGE

SERVICES FOR STUDENTS WITH DISABILITIES

LOCATION

East Mesa Campus - DASR Room 206A

HOURS

Monday-Friday: 8am - 5pm

COST | ELIGIBILITY

Students who are outlined in the Americans with Disabilities Act (ADA) of 1990 and Section 504 of the Rehabilitation Act of 1973.

SERVICES PROVIDED Provides accommodations to DACC students who are eligible.

DONA ANA COMMUNITY COLLEGE

COMPUTER LAB

LOCATION

Central Campus Room 85

HOURS

Monday-Thursday: 8am - 10pm
Friday: 8am - 5pm
Saturday: 9am - 5pm
Sunday: 1pm - 5pm

COST | ELIGIBILITY

To all currently enrolled students

SERVICES PROVIDED Copy machine, Internet and standard computer programs available.

DONA ANA COMMUNITY COLLEGE

STUDENT SUCCESS CENTER

LOCATION

Central Campus Room 83
East Mesa Campus Academic Resources Building
Room 201

HOURS

Monday-Thursday: 8am - 6pm
Friday: 8am - 5pm
Saturday: 10am - 3pm
East Mesa location is not open on Saturdays

COST | ELIGIBILITY

Students currently enrolled at DACC

SERVICES PROVIDED Free tutoring sessions in most subject areas. Sessions are up to one hour Tutors can also assist in writing papers.

DONA ANA COMMUNITY COLLEGE

COLLEGE CAREER SERVICES

LOCATION

Central Campus Room 109
East Mesa DASR Room 111

HOURS

Monday-Friday: 8am - 5pm

COST | ELIGIBILITY

Students currently enrolled at DACC

SERVICES PROVIDED To assist the student, the college, and the community with the development of their employment strategies. To create an environment to explore and address current employment issues.

DONA ANA COMMUNITY COLLEGE

COLLEGE ADVISING SERVICES

LOCATION
East Mesa Campus - Room 103

HOURS
Monday-Friday: 8:30am - 4pm

COST | ELIGIBILITY
Students currently enrolled at DACC

SERVICES PROVIDED   Provides advising and clarification on degree plans.

VOLUNTEER
OPPORTUNITIES

COMMUNITY OF HOPE

LOCATION

999 West Amador Ave.
 Las Cruces, NM
88005

HOURS

Hours vary
Call for more info

SERVICES PROVIDED

Housing and Homeless Prevention Services
•**Shelter Plus Care:** Individual apartments for homeless people with disabilities and their families
•**Abode Permanent Housing:** A group home for the chronically homeless
•**Transitional Housing:** Subsidized rent to help families stabilize after becoming homeless
•**Sue's Place:** A group residence for chronically homeless women (Coming soon 2013)
•**Veterans Housing:** Ongoing rental assistance for Veterans at a 20-unit complex with classes and activities five days a week; One-time assistance available to homeless vets for security deposit, first month's rent, homeless prevention, and utility assistance.
•As available, New Home Set-ups for those in housing programs
     -Furniture
     -Household goods
     -Miscellaneous supplies

VOLUNTEER DUTIES

•Organizing our donation rooms
•Trainings in our Resource Room (for example, if you are good with computers, holding a computer training class, or art, or exercise, etc).

JARDIN DE LOS NIÑOS

LOCATION

999 W. Amador Ave.
Las Cruces, NM
88001

SERVICES PROVIDED

•Therapeutic childcare services
•Specialized care for developmental delays
•Early learning
•Experiential learning
•Comprehensive family services
•Parenting support group sessions
•Parents as partners in the classroom
•Family case management
•Progress reviews/home visits
•Family advocacy
•On-site health assessments and medical care

VOLUNTEER DUTIES

Volunteer at La Tienda de Jardin
•Assist customers
•Run the cash register
•Sort donated items
•Stage the displays

SNAP SPAY AND NEUTER SOUTHWEST NEW MEXICO

LOCATION

365 Avenida de Mesilla
Las Cruces, NM 88005

HOURS

Tuesday- Friday:
11am - 2pm

SERVICES PROVIDED

To prevent the suffering and death of
dogs and cats due to overpopulation.

VOLUNTEER DUTIES

•Office duty
•Administrative help
•Volunteer at one of SNAP's many fundraisers
•Bi-lingual volunteers are needed as well

MESILLA VALLEY HOSPICE

LOCATION

299 E. Montana
Las Cruces, NM
88005

HOURS

Monday - Saturday:
8am- 5tpm

SERVICES PROVIDED

•Prevention and control of pain and other symptoms
•Regular visits from the Hospice team including RN, CNA, Social Worker, Counselors and Spiritual support if requested
•Medications, equipment and supplies related to the terminal illness
•Emotional and spiritual support
•Volunteers who can provide relief time for the family
•Therapists as needed
•24 hour On Call response 7 days a week
•Liereavement Program

VOLUNTEER DUTIES

See website:
www.mvhospice.org/volunteer.php

HABITAT FOR HUMANITY

LOCATION

720 N Santa Fe Las
Cruces, NM 88001

HOURS

Call for appointment
information

SERVICES PROVIDED

•Working to make a difference in the lives of those living in substandard housing conditions in Mesilla Valley.
•Helping families get into good housing conditions
•Also changing the outlook members of these families have on life.

VOLUNTEER DUTIES

For a list of duties please visit:
www.lascruceshabitat.org/you-can-help/

GLBTQ CENTER

LOCATION

1210 N. Main St.
Las Cruces, NM
88001

HOURS

Monday-Sunday:
12pm - 8pm

SERVICES PROVIDED

•Support groups
•Social activities
•Referrals for legal, medical & psychology services
•A LGBTQ lending library
•Free Wi- Fi
•Computers to use
•Community information

VOLUNTEER DUTIES

•LGBTQ event volunteering
•Office help
•Big Brother, Big Sister

LA CASA

LOCATION

800 S Walnut St
Las Cruces, NM
88001

HOURS

Monday-Friday:
7:30am - 5:30pm

SERVICES PROVIDED

Offers programs that help and support individuals with and families who are victims of abuse or domestic violence.
•Emergency Shelter Program
•Non- resident Program
•Children's Program
•Men's Program
•Transitional Housing
•Satellite Program
•Parenting Programs
•Education and Prevention
•Civil Legal Services

VOLUNTEER DUTIES

•Children's activities and projects
•Shelter volunteer
•General office work
•Special events and tabling
•Yard work and maintenance

SAFE HAVEN ANIMAL SANCTUARY

LOCATION

840-D El Paseo
Las Cruces, NM
88001

SERVICES PROVIDED

•Sanctuary provides temporary shelter, food, and space for homeless pets in the Dona Ana County Community.

•SHAS operates a Thrift Shop located at 840-D El Paseo Las Cruces, New Mexico 88001 (575)-541-4942

  -Monday-Saturday 9am - 5pm

  Sunday 11am - 4pm

•Donations of salable items keep the store thriving and proceeds   from the sale of donated items support the animals at the sanctuary.

•Donations of dog and cat food as well as cat litter can also be taken to the store for transport to the sanctuary

VOLUNTEER DUTIES

Please visit this website for a complete list of volunteer duties available.
http://www.safehavenanimalsanctuary. net/volunteer.htm

EL CALDITO SOUP KITCHEN

LOCATION

999 West Amador
Las Cruces, NM
88005

HOURS

Monday-Friday:
8am - 1pmt

SERVICES PROVIDED

Grade A food establishment dedicated to providing free midday meals to the homeless and poverty- afflicted population of Las Cruces.

VOLUNTEER DUTIES

For a full list of Kitchen Volunteer duties available please visit the website.
http://elcaldito.wordpress.com/volunteers/

BRANIGAN LIBRARY

LOCATION

200 E. Picacho Ave.
Las Cruces, NM
88001

HOURS

Mon-Thur: 9am - 8pm
Fri-Sat: 10am - 6pm
Sun: 1pm - 5pm

SERVICES PROVIDED

Branigan Library offers books, magazines, newspapers, DVD's, audiobooks, as well as downloadable audiobooks
•Offers computers
•Access to powerful research databases, family programming, movies, and much more.
•Computer lab with internet access, many popular computer programs, a laser printer and copy machines accessible

VOLUNTEER DUTIES

Include but not limited to:
•Help re-shelving books that are returned to the library
•Repairing books
•Working in the computer lab

BRANIGAN CULTURAL CENTER

LOCATION

501 N. Main St.
Las Cruces, NM
88001

HOURS

Tuesday-Saturdays:
9am - 4:30pmt

SERVICES PROVIDED

Dedicated to engaging out visitors in rich heritage of the Southwest and the world at large through artistic, cultural, and historical exhibitions and programs.
•Permanently hosts a local history exhibit and cultural exhibits
•Offers educational programs, classes, concerts, and other special events.

VOLUNTEER DUTIES

For a full list of Volunteer Positions in the Museums please visit the website.

MUSEUM OF ART

LOCATION

491 N. Main St.
Las Cruces, NM
88001

HOURS

Tuesday-Saturday:
9am - 4:30pm

SERVICES PROVIDED

•Hosts Changing contemporary art exhibits, including national, international, juried, traveling, and invitational exhibits.
•Hosts extensive art studio class program for all ages

VOLUNTEER DUTIES

For a full list of Volunteer Positions in the Museums please visit the website.

MUSEUM OF NATURE & SCIENCE

LOCATION

450 N. Water St.
Las Cruces, NM
88001

HOURS

Tuesday-Saturday:
9am - 4:30pm

SERVICES PROVIDED

To inspire curiosity about the sciences that facilitate life-long learning.

Exhibitions:
• Desert Life
• Permian Trackways
• Light & Space

Activity and Programs include Behind the Scenes tour of the Nature Center, Dinos A-Z, Magic Planet Show, Night at the Museum (Overnight), Desert Trek and so much more.

VOLUNTEER DUTIES

For a full list of Volunteer Positions in the Museums please visit the website.

RAILROAD MUSEUM

LOCATION

351 N. Mesilla St.
Las Cruces, NM
88005

HOURS

Thursday-Saturday:
9am - 4pm

SERVICES PROVIDED

Interprets and Displays Las Cruces
Railroad History.
•Historical Trains to view
•Historical Train Parts on display
•Three model Train layout to tour and
experience yourself

VOLUNTEER DUTIES

For a full list of Volunteer Positions in the
Museums please visit the website.

MESILLA VALLEY BOSQUE STATE PARK

LOCATION

5000 Calle del Norte
Mesilla, NM
88046

HOURS

Wednesday-Sunday:
7tam - 4pm

SERVICES PROVIDED

Visitors have many opportunities to view
wildlife in natural surroundings while
strolling one of the self-guided nature
trails while enjoying a fun ranger-led tour.
•Birding
•Hiking
•Photography opportunities
•Wildlife viewing
•Natural wildlife education

VOLUNTEER DUTIES

•Campground Host
•Visitor Center Associate
•Maintenance Volunteer
•Interpretive Assistant
•Boating Safety Instructor
•Special Events Coordinator
•Archaeology Site Steward
•Presentation and Tour Guide

CASA DE PEREGRINOS

LOCATION

999 W. Amador Ave.
Suite F
Las Cruces, NM 88005

HOURS

Mon-Wed-Fri:
9am - 11am
1pm - 2pm

SERVICES PROVIDED

A nonprofit & nondenominational that offers:
•Emergency food program
•Provides free food supplemental groceries to individuals and families at risk of hunger in Las Cruces and Dona Ana counties

VOLUNTEER DUTIES

•Bagging and assembling Casa's standard food packs
•Bagging fresh produce
•Sorting and shelving canned and dry foods
•Interviewing clients
•Filling carts for clients
•Write thank-you letters
•Write grant proposals
•Update Microsoft Access
•Help plan and carry out fundraising events

NM FARM & RANCH HERITAGE MUSEUM

LOCATION

4100 Dripping
Springs Rd
Las Cruces, NM 88011

HOURS

Mon-Sat: 9am - 5pm
Sunday: 12pm - 5pm

SERVICES PROVIDED

Several hours of fun combined with learning.
With many exhibits and demonstrations indoors and outside
•Demonstrations include milking and blacksmithing
•With a variety of livestock tours available

VOLUNTEER DUTIES

Processes volunteer education first.
•Education volunteer
•Training classes
•Mentoring
•Tours
•Event Volunteering

"

TAKING CARE OF BUSINESS

HAVING FUN
CAN COEXIST PEACEFULLY.
"

–MEGAN KETELBOETER
NMSU ALUMNI

DIRECTORY

A | DACC **ADVISING CENTER**

☎ (575) 528-7272

🏠 DACC East Mesa Campus, Room 103

💻 www.dacc.nmsu.edu/advising

NMSU **AQUATIC CENTER**

☎ (575) 646-3518

🏠 Stewart Street between Locust and Williams Ave.

💻 www.recsport.nmsu.edu/nat

Associate Director: Danois Montoya

☎ (575) 646-1708

✉ danois@nmsu.edu

B | **BARNES & NOBLE CAFE**

☎ (575) 646-4431

🏠 1400 E. University Ave., Las Cruces, NM, 88003

💻 www.nmsu-lascruces.bncollege.com

Store Manager: Joanna Koliba

NMSU **BLACK PROGRAMS**

☎ (575) 646-4208

🏠 Main Campus, Garcia Annex, Room 135

💻 www.nmsu.edu/~blackpro

Director: Festus Addo-Yobo

☎ (575) 646-4208

✉ festus@nmsu.edu

BRANIGAN CULTURAL CENTER

- (575) 541-2154
- 501 N. Main St., Las Cruces, NM 88001
- www.las-cruces.org/museums

Volunteer Coordinator: Julia Hansen

- (575) 541-2322
- jhansen@las-cruces.org

BRANIGAN LIBRARY

- (575) 528-4000
- 200 E. Picacho Ave., Las Cruces, NM 88001
- www.library.las-cruces.org/

Volunteer Coordinator: Genevieve Kirk

- (575) 528-3035
- gkirk@las-cruces.org

DACC CAREER SERVICES

- (575) 527-7538
- DACC, Central Campus, DAMA Room 109
- www.dacc.nmsu.edu/cs

Student Career Resource Coordinator: Cynthia Brown

- (575) 527-7536
- jobsquad@nmsu.edu

CASA DE PEREGRINOS

- (575) 523-5542
- 999 W. Amador Ave. Suite F, Las Cruces, NM 88005
- www.casadeperegrinos.org
- casadepere@yahoo.com

CENTER FOR THE ARTS

🏠 Corner of University and Espina

💻 www.nmsutheatre.com

Director of Development: Jim Grammer

📞 (575) 646-3587

✉ jgrammar@nmsu.edu

COMMUNITY OF HOPE

📞 (575) 523-2219

🏠 999 W. Amador Ave., Las Cruces, NM 88005

💻 www.mvcommunityofhope.org

Executive Director: Nicole Martinez

✉ hope@zianet.com

DACC COMPUTER LAB

📞 Central (575) 527-7561 East Mesa (575) 528-7265

🏠 DACC Central Campus, Room 85

💻 www.dacc.nmsu.edu/computer-labs

NMSU COOPERATIVE EDUCATION

📞 (575) 646-4115

🏠 Main Campus, Garcia Annex, 2nd Floor Room 224

💻 www.careerservices.nmsu.edu/coop

Coordinator: Albina Armijo

📞 (575) 646-7936

✉ alarmijo@nmsu.edu

C   DACC COUNSELING & WELLNESS CENTER

- ☎ (575) 527-7548
- 🏠 DACC Main Building, Room 117
- 💻 www.dacc.nmsu.edu/counseling

NMSU CREATIVE MEDIA INSTITUE

- ☎ (575) 646-4115
- 🏠 Main Campus, Milton Hall, Room 172B
- 💻 www.creativemedia.nmsu.edu

Department Head: James Maupin

- ☎ (575) 646-2260
- ✉ jmaupin@nmsu.edu

NMSU CRIMSON SCHOLARS

- ☎ (575) 646-2542
- 🏠 Main Campus, Conroy Honors Building, Room 104
- 💻 www.honors.nmsu.edu/crimson-scholars/

D   DACC DUAL CREDIT OFFICE

- ☎ (575) 528-7256
- 🏠 DACC East Mesa, Student Resources Building, Room 101B
- 💻 www.dacc.nmsu.edu/DualCredit

E   EL CALDITO SOUP KITCHEN

- ☎ (575) 525-3831
- 🏠 999 W. Amador Ave., Las Cruces, NM 88005
- 💻 www.elcaldito.wordpress.org

Volunteer Coordinator: Donna Wood

- ✉ elcaldito@yahoo.com

FAMILY RESOURCE CENTER

- ☎ (575) 646-2065
- 🏠 4145 Sam Steel Way, Las Cruces, NM 88003
  C-100 Cervantes Village near Children's Village
- 💻 www.aces.nmsu.edu/familresourcecenter/

Department Head: Esther Devall

- ☎ (575) 646-1161
- ✉ edevall@nmsu.edu

DACC FINANCIAL AID & SCHOLARSHIPS

- ☎ (575) 527-7696
- 🏠 3400 S. Espina, Las Cruces, NM 88003
- 💻 www.dacc.nmsu.edu/fa

GLBTQ CENTER

- 🏠 1210 N. Main St., Las Cruces, NM 88001
- 💻 www.newmexicoglbtqcenters.org

HABITAT FOR HUMANITY

- ☎ (575) 525-0475
- 🏠 720 N. Santa Fe, Las Cruces, NM 88001
- 💻 www.lascruceshabitat.org

President: Pete Lucero

NMSU INDIAN RESOURCE DEVELOPMENT PROGRAM

- ☎ (575) 646-1347
- 🏠 Main Campus, Gerald Thomas Hall, Room 263
- 💻 www.aces.nmsu.edu/academics/ird

Director: Joe Graham

- ☎ (575) 646-1347
- ✉ graham@nmsu.edu

J | JARDIN DE LOS NINOS

- ☎ (575) 522-2111
- 🏠 999 W. Amador Ave., Las Cruces, NM 88001
- 💻 www.jardinlc.org

Shirley Jaquez

- ☎ (575) 522-2111
- ✉ shirleyjaquez@hotmail.com

L | LA CASA

- ☎ (575) 526-2819
- 🏠 800 S. Walnut St., Las Cruces, NM 88001
- 💻 www.lacasainc.org

Volunteer Coordinator: Laura Arriaga

- ☎ (575) 526-2819

DACC LIBRARY & MEDIA CENTER

- ☎ Central (575) 527-7555 East Mesa (575) 528-7260
- 🏠 Central Campus, 2nd Floor of Learning Resources Building Room 260

  East Mesa Campus, 2nd Floor Academic Resources Building Room 203
- 💻 www.dacc.nmsu.edu/library

M | NMSU MATH SUCCESS CENTER

- ☎ (575) 646-5743
- 🏠 Main Campus, Walden Hall, Room 101
- 💻 www.math.nmsu.edu/msc

Specialist Instructor: Alex Alvarado

- ☎ (575) 646-5743
- ✉ rodralva@nmsu.edu

M | # MESILLA VALLEY BOSQUE STATE PARK

📞 (575) 523-4398

🏠 5000 Calle del Norte, Mesilla, NM 88046

💻 www.emnrd.state.nm.us/spd/mesillavalleystatepark

Superintendent: Janet Kirwan

✉ janet.kirwan@state.nm.us

MESILLA VALLEY HOSPICE

📞 (575) 525-5757

🏠 299 E. Montana, Las Cruces, NM 88005

💻 www.mvhospice.org

Lorraine Padilla

📞 (575) 525-5757

✉ lpadilla@mvhospice.org

MUSEUM OF ART

📞 (575) 541-2137

🏠 491 N. Main St., Las Cruces, NM 88001

💻 www.las-cruces.org/museums

Volunteer Coordinator: Julia Hansen

📞 (575) 541-2322

✉ jhansen@las-cruces.org

MUSEUM OF NATURE & SCIENCE

📞 (575) 522-3120

🏠 450 N. Water St., Las Cruces, NM 88001

💻 www.las-cruces.org/museums

Volunteer Coordinator: Julia Hansen

📞 (575) 541-2322

✉ jhansen@las-cruces.org

N | NEW MEXICO FARM & RANCH HERTIAGE MUSEUM

☎ (575) 522-4100

🏠 4100 Dripping Springs Rd., Las Cruces, NM 88011

💻 www.nmfarmandranchmuseum.org

Volunteer Coordinator: Debbie Holderby

☎ (575) 522-4100 ext. 116

✉ debra.holderby@state.nm.us

R | RAILROAD MUSEUM

☎ (575) 647-4480

🏠 351 N. Mesilla St., Las Cruces, NM 88005

💻 www.las-cruces.org/museums

Volunteer Coordinator: Julia Hansen

☎ (575) 514-2322

✉ jhansen@las-cruces.org

S | SAFE HAVEN ANIMAL SANCTUARY

☎ (575) 527-4555

🏠 840-D El Paseo, Las Cruces, NM 88001

💻 www.safehavenanimalsanctuary.net

Sanctuary Manager: Jeff Barker

✉ safehaven@nightfury.com

DACC SERVICES FOR STUDENTS WITH DISABILITIES

☎ (575) 527-7648

🏠 DACC East Mesa, Room 206A

💻 www.dacc.nmsu.edu/ssd

SNAP: SPAY & NEUTER SOUTHWEST NEW MEXICO

📞 (575) 524-9265

🏠 365 Avenida de Mesilla, Las Cruces, NM 88005

💻 www.snapnewmexico.org

President: Sherry Gara

📞 (575) 524-9265

✉ snapnm@zianet.com

NMSU STUDENT HEALTH CENTER

📞 (575) 646-1512

🏠 365 Avenida de Mesilla, Las Cruces, NM 88005

💻 www.wellness.nmsu.edu/shc

Staff Physician/Medica Director: Benjamin Diven

📞 (575) 646-1512

NMSU STUDENT JUDICIAL AFFAIRS

📞 (575) 646-1722

🏠 Main Campus, Corbett Center, Suite 230

💻 www.deanofstudents.nmsu.edu/student-judicial-services

Coordinator: Angela Arvizo

📞 (575) 646-1722

✉ aarvizo@nmsu.edu

DACC STUDENT RESOURCE TESTING CENTER

📞 (575) 527-7569S

🏠 DACC East Mesa, DASR Room 105

💻 www.dacc.nmsu.edu/testing

DACC STUDENT SUCCESS CENTER

🏠 Central Campus, Room 83

East Mesa Campus, Academic Resources Building Room 201

💻 www.dacc.nmsu.edu/SSC/tutorials-resources

NMSU STUDENT JUDICIAL AFFAIRS

📞 (575) 646-1722

🏠 Main Campus, Corbett Center, Suite 230

💻 www.deanofstudents.nmsu.edu/student-judicial-services

Coordinator: Angela Arvizo

📞 (575) 646-1722

✉ aarvizo@nmsu.edu

NMSU STUDENT SUPPORT SERVICES TRIO PROGRAM (SSS)

📞 (575) 646-1336

🏠 Main Campus, Hardman Hall Room 210

💻 www.trio.nmsu.edu/sss

Program Coordinator: Johana Bencomo

📞 (575) 646-3340

✉ jbencomo@nmsu.edu

NMSU STUDY ABROAD OFFICE

📞 (575) 646-5107

🏠 Main Campus, Garcia Annex, Room 238

💻 www.studyabroad.nmsu.edu

Coordinator: Kristi Drexler

📞 (575) 646-4528

✉ kdrexler@nmsu.edu

U | NMSU UNIVERSITY MUSEUM

☎ (575) 646-5161

🏠 Main Campus, Kent Hall

💻 www.nmsu.edu/museum

Museum Director: Monte McCrossin

☎ (575) 646-5161

✉ mmccross@nmsu.edu

W | NMSU WRITING CENTER

☎ (575) 646-5297

🏠 Main Campus, Clara Belle Williams Hall, Room 102

💻 www.nmsu.edu/~english/resources/writingcenter

Z | NMSU ZUHL LIBRARY COPY CENTER

☎ (575) 646-6910

🏠 Main Campus, Zuhl Library, 1st Floor

💻 www.lib.nmsu.edu/depts/accserv/copycenter

Jeanette Smith

☎ (575) 646-7492

✉ jcsmith@lib.nmsu.edu

PHILIP HERNANDEZ is a producer, entrepreneur, author, and college instructor from Las Cruces, NM.

Currently, he is the President of the Dona Ana Theatre Association and the Editor of Behind The Curtain.

He has published two books, acted for cable television, founded several organizations, owned a successful art gallery, worked for Disney, and lead some of the most-attended and expansive 'Halloween-themed' events in the city.

Believing that the key to educating students and to developing communities is through hands-on activities, art, and culture he brings people and mediums together in interesting ways. His aspires to devote his life to help sustain, develop, and promote the arts.

In May 2012 he graduated from New Mexico State University with a Bachelor of Science in Hotel, Restaurant, and Tourism Management with a minor in both English and Business Management.

www.ingramcontent.com/pod-product-compliance
Lightning Source LLC
Chambersburg PA
CBHW081145290526

45795CB00006B/2374